IN MEMO
OF THE MICHELIN
AND WORKMEN WHO !
FOR THEIR C

AMIENS
BEFORE AND DURING THE WAR

Copyright 1919 by Michelin & Cie.

All rights of translation, adaptation or reproduction (in part or whole) reserved in all countries.

PANORAMA
OF AMIENS.

ORIGIN

In the days of the Gauls, Amiens, then known as Samarobriva, or " Bridge over the Somme," was the capital of the Ambiani, a tribe of Belgian origin. Later it passed under Roman domination, and in the fifth century under that of the Franks. Christianity was first preached there at the beginning of the fourth century, by St. Firmin, first bishop and martyr of Amiens. After the death of Charlemagne, the town became the property of the counts and bishops. The latter were unable to defend it against the Normans, who ravaged it on several occasions. In 1185, it was annexed to the royal dominions, under Philippe Auguste. On account of its position, between Paris and the sea, Amiens acquired great importance at that time, and became the store-house for all the goods sent down the river Somme for distribution over the whole of northern France. The manufacture of cloth and linen, and the preparation of " woad " (vegetable dye-stuff used on a very large scale in the Middle Ages) caused Amiens to become as rich and flourishing as the Flemish towns.

BRIEF DESCRIPTION

Built on the Somme, at the confluence of that river with its tributaries, the Avre and the Selle, and at the junction of nine different railways, Amiens is divided, topographically, into three parts.

To the south, is the higher or new town, bounded by two lines of boulevards planted with fine chestnut and linden trees, and occupying the site of the ancient ramparts. Between this double belt, rise the suburbs of Noyon, Henri-Ville, and Beauvais, with their straight streets, handsome mansions, and brick-built residences.

In the centre, extending as far as the river Somme, is the business part of the town, containing the shops, public buildings, and ancient monuments.

On the right bank, from the Somme to the lateral canal, which describes a large semi-circle between the " ports d'Amont et d'Aval," lies old Amiens or the lower town, with its narrow winding streets, wooden houses, workshops and factories, situated between the many arms of the river.

This quarter is dominated by the ancient citadel, and prolonged by the new suburbs of St. Maurice and St. Pierre, where the working population of the spinning mills and factories lives.

GERMAN FOOT-SOLDIERS ENTERING AMIENS.

AMIENS DURING THE WAR

Twice during the War, the strategical importance of Amiens caused it to become the objective of the German armies.

How the Germans occupied Amiens in 1914

After the battle of Charleroi, and in consequence of von Kluck's manifest intention to outflank the left wing of the retreating Allies, Amiens became threatened.

At that time a group of divisions under General d'Amade, comprising the 81st, 82nd, 84th, and 88th territorials, and the 61st and 62nd reserves, was stationed between Dunkirk and Maubeige, with orders to check enemy cavalry raids.

However, the front allotted to these troops was so long that they formed merely a thin curtain, which was obliged to retire before the approach of the first German army.

Amiens was then occupied by Moroccan troops, which were hurriedly despatched in the direction of Comon and Villers-Bretonneux, to organise defensive positions.

General d'Amade arrived on August 27th.

"NACH PARIS" GERMAN FIELD KITCHEN.

His territorial divisions were sent by train to a point below the town, with orders to prevent the Germans from crossing the Somme. On the same day, the 61st and 62nd reserve divisions marched towards Péronne, their ultimate destination being south of the Somme. However, on debouching from Bapaume, they had an extremely violent engagement with a German army corps. The battle continued until the following day, eventually turning in favour of the enemy, and the two divisions were thrown back northwards.

Further to the east, General Sordet's cavalry corps, which was supporting the left wing of the British army to the east of the line Le Catelet-Roisel, sought to check the German advance, but was unable to prevent the enemy from reaching the outskirts of Péronne on the evening of the 27th. The cavalry accordingly withdrew to the south of the Somme.

On the 28th, the enemy took Péronne, and marched on Amiens. The cavalry corps fell back towards the south.

On the 29th, General Maunoury, in command of a new army (the 6th), made the necessary dispositions to prevent his left from being out-flanked, and to check the enemy, whose advance-guards nearest Amiens had reached Bray-sur-Somme, Chuignolles and Framerville. In the first line were placed:

A brigade of Moroccan chasseurs;
The 14th division of the 7th corps, from Alsace, which had detrained at Villers-Bretonneux on the 27th;
The 45th and 55th battalions of chasseurs.

On the right, in the direction of Nesle, were units of the 55th division.

The French attacked during the morning, inflicting heavy losses on the enemy, and capturing the village of Proyart. At the same time, the four territorial divisions moved up the Somme and established themselves in Amiens.

In the evening, the enemy counter-attacked in superior numbers. The 7th corps lost the positions won that morning, and withdrew to the south. From that moment, the town became exposed; the territorials evacuated it on the 30th, during the day, their rear-guard having several skirmishes with enemy patrols near Cagny.

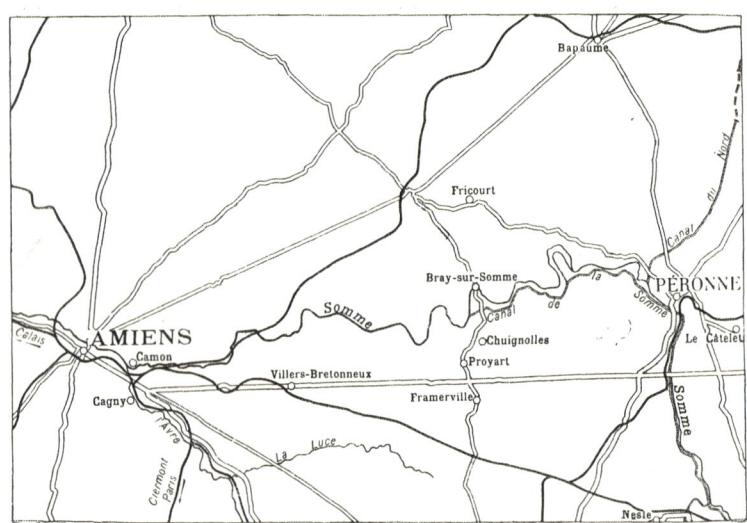

Retreat of the German Artillery (PLACE DE LA GARE).

Occupation of Amiens

The enemy entered the town on August 31st, and immediately made requisitions of all kinds, including food and money. These requisitions, of a total value of about 500,000 frs., had to be complied with the same day.

Twelve town councillors and the Attorney-General were taken as hostages, and were only released on September 11th after much anxious suspense and annoyance.

At first, the Imperial army merely passed through Amiens on its forced march " nach Paris." From the 1st to the 9th of September there were practically no Germans in the town. Occasionally, officers paid hurried visits, exacting further requisitions, and breaking open the safes of the Savings Banks.

On September 9th, a garrison was installed, and a major appointed Kommandant of the town. Injunctions, prohibitions, and requisitions became more severe immediately. It was forbidden to be in the streets after 8 p.m., or to sell newspapers. Motor vehicles were seized, and Frenchmen residing in Amiens who had not been mobilised, were ordered to the Citadel. Two-thirds of them were eventually released, but about a thousand young men were sent away into captivity. They had scarcely left, when the Germans withdrew precipitately from the town.

On September 11th, only a few laggards remained. The effect of the defeat on the Marne was making itself felt.

On the 12th, General d'Amade's advance-guards, returning from the vicinity of Rouen, re-entered the town and took a few prisoners. The territorial divisions occupied Amiens until the 17th, when they left in a north-easterly direction, taking part at the end of the month in the battles at Péronne and Fricourt, which again fixed the front-line positions. Relieved and protected by lines of trenches, Amiens was safe from the enemy until March, 1918.

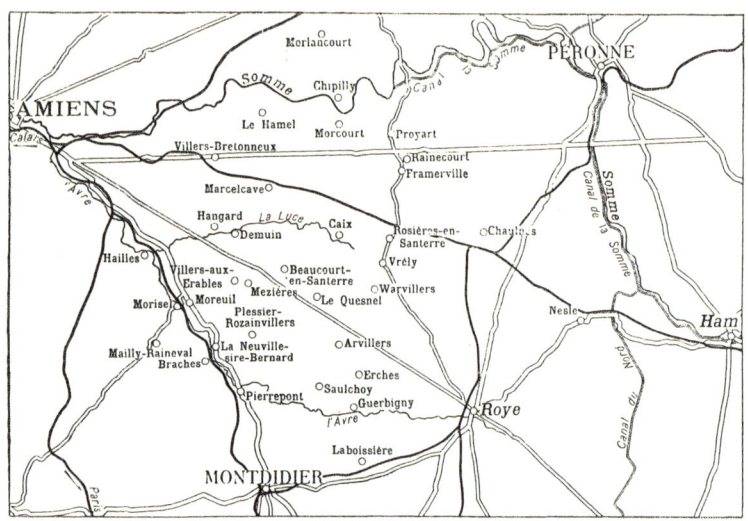

How Amiens was saved in 1918

In 1918, a new onrush of the German armies brought them almost to the gates of Amiens. On March 21st, Ludendorff opened his great offensive by hurling a million fanatical troops against the 5th British Army. Bapaume, Péronne, and Montdidier fell in a few days; a stretch of territory, sixty kilometres broad, was occupied by the enemy, who captured enormous booty. For a moment, the road to long-coveted Paris seemed open. Thanks, however, to the prodigious resistance of the French troops, who barred the valley of the Oise, the breach was promptly closed. It was then that the enemy returned to his first objective, *i.e.*, the separation of the two Allied armies. On March 27th the Germans hurled themselves at Amiens, which formed the hinge of the Allies' front.

For several days the struggle continued to be extremely violent; the enemy gained some ground, but was unable to break through. Démuin, Moreuil, Marcelcave, and Hangard were fiercely disputed until March 31st. These villages mark the extreme line reached by the enemy—*i.e.*, 17 kilometres from Amiens.

On April 4th, the Germans attacked again, determined to break through at all costs. Against the French front alone, 15 kilometres in length, eleven divisions were hurled. Crossing to the left bank of the Avre, they took the villages of Morisel and Mailly-Raineval from Debeney's army, and threatened the railway from Clermont to Amiens, which was their objective. At Hangard, the British, shoulder to shoulder with the French, repulsed all attacks. Further to the north, they withdrew to the west of Hamel, and during the night were forced back to the Villers-Bretonneux plateau. However, vigorous counter-attacks enabled them to win back the lost ground next day.

From the 15th to the 19th of April, local offensives enabled the French to clear the railway. However, the Germans had not given up their plan, and after a violent bombardment during the night, they again attacked, on April 24th at 5 a.m., the Franco-British junction between Villers-Bretonneux, held by the British, and a point west of Moreuil. Villers-Bretonneux fell, but the French troops were able to hold Hailles. Bayonet fighting took place in the streets of Hangard, which was lost during the night. On the morning of the 26th, the French and British counter-attacked from Villers-Bretonneux to the valley of the Luce, and drove the enemy back to their starting-point of the 24th.

RAILWAY STATION, ST. ROCH.

Once again, Amiens had escaped, but it remained within range of the German heavy guns. The town, which had previously suffered on various occasions from air bombardments, was now continuously and violently bombarded, especially by artillery, from April to June. Ruins accumulated in the town and suburbs, both of which had been evacuated by the inhabitants on April 9th.

Liberation of Amiens

The final liberation of the town began on August 8th, with the great Allied offensive. The 4th British army (Rawlinson) and the 1st French army (Debeney), in liaison on the road from Amiens to Roye, attacked at dawn from Braches to Morlancourt, the respective positions of Von der Marwitz and Von Hutier. The Australian and Canadian infantry, supported by numerous tanks, completely surprised the panic-stricken enemy. In a few hours, Villers-Bretonneux was cleared, and in the evening the British reached Chépilly, Framerville, Caix, and Beaucourt-en-Santerre.

To the south, the French, by clever manœuvring, advanced 8 kilometres, and established themselves on the line La-Neuville-Sire-Bernard-Plessier-Rozainvillers-Villers-aux-Érables. That night, Debeney and Rawlinson joined hands at Mézières, both having captured enormous booty.

On the 9th, progress was maintained, in spite of the growing resistance of the enemy. The British took the line of exterior defensive works of Amiens, and reached Le Quesnel, Rosières-en-Santerre, Rainecourt, and Morocourt. Debeney encircled Montdidier; to the north, his troops captured Arvillers and Pierrepont, while to the south, an attack made in the evening forced the enemy to evacuate the town on the following morning and to retreat to La Bossière. During the same day (10th), the British captured Proyart and approached Chaulnes.

From that moment Amiens was safe from further aggression, as the Germans, harried by the victorious Allied armies, retreated each day.

230mm. GUN WHICH BOMBARDED AMIENS. CAPTURED BY AUSTRALIANS. RANGE: 30 MILES.

VILLE D'AMIENS

Douze otages pris parmi les membres du Conseil Municipal auxquels s'est joint M. le Procureur-Général, répondent sur leur vie de l'engagement pris par la Municipalité qu'aucun acte d'hostilité ne sera commis par la population contre les troupes allemandes.

Le 31 Août 1914.

Le Sénateur-Maire,

A. FIQUET.

(Translation)

Twelve hostages chosen from the town councillors, and the Attorney General, will answer with their lives for the undertaking entered into by the Municipality that no hostile act will be committed by the population against the German troops.

31st August, 1914.

Senator-Mayor: A. FIQUET.

EFFECTS OF AN INCENDIARY SHELL NEAR THE BOULEVARDS

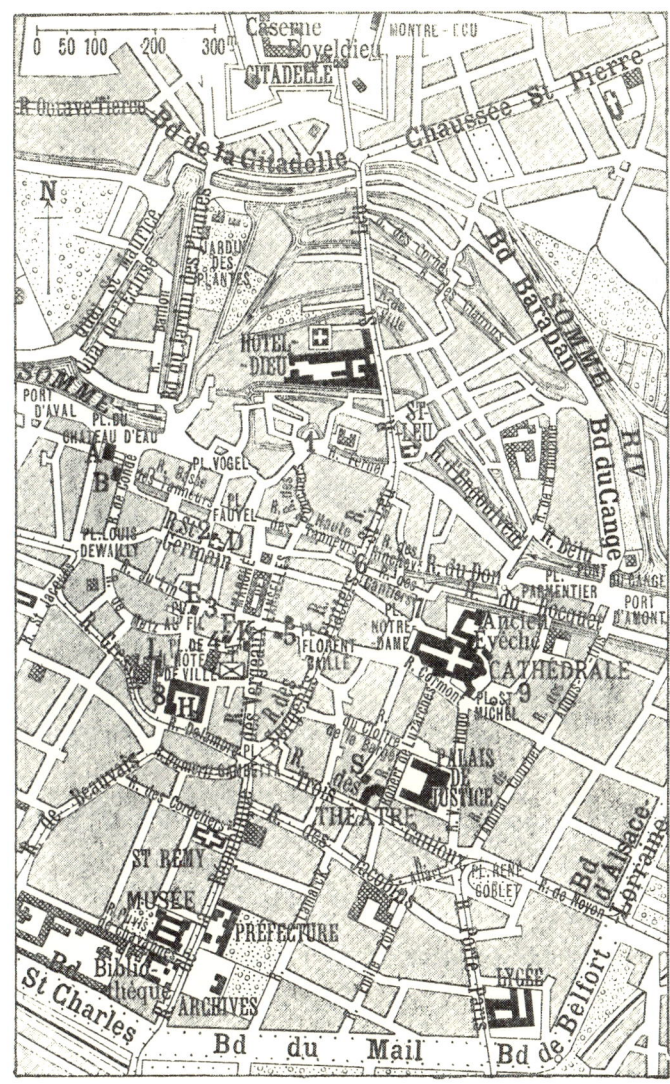

CENTRE OF AMIENS

1. Place Samarobrive.
2. Rue Pingré.
3. Rue des Chaudronniers.
4. Passage Gossart.
5. Rue St.-Martin.
6. Rue du Bloc.
7. Rue St. Firmin the Confessor.
8. Rue de la Malmaison.
9. Rue de Metz-l'Évêque.

A — Old Water-Works (Museum); B — Hôtel Morgan de Belloy; D — St. Germain's Church; E — Belfry; F — House of the White Gable; H — Hôtel de Ville; K — Archer's House; L — Bailliage; S — Logis du Gouverneur du Roi.

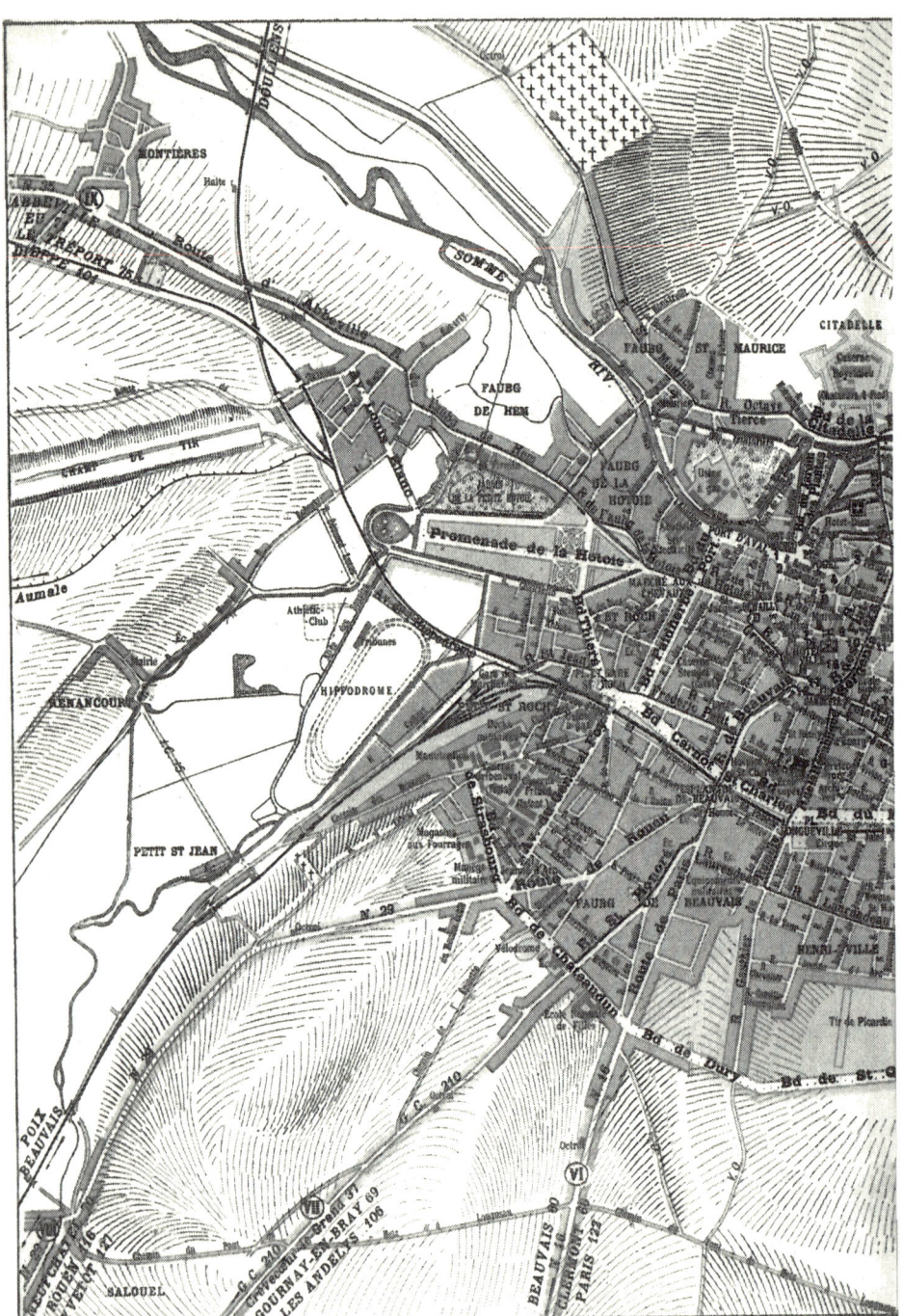

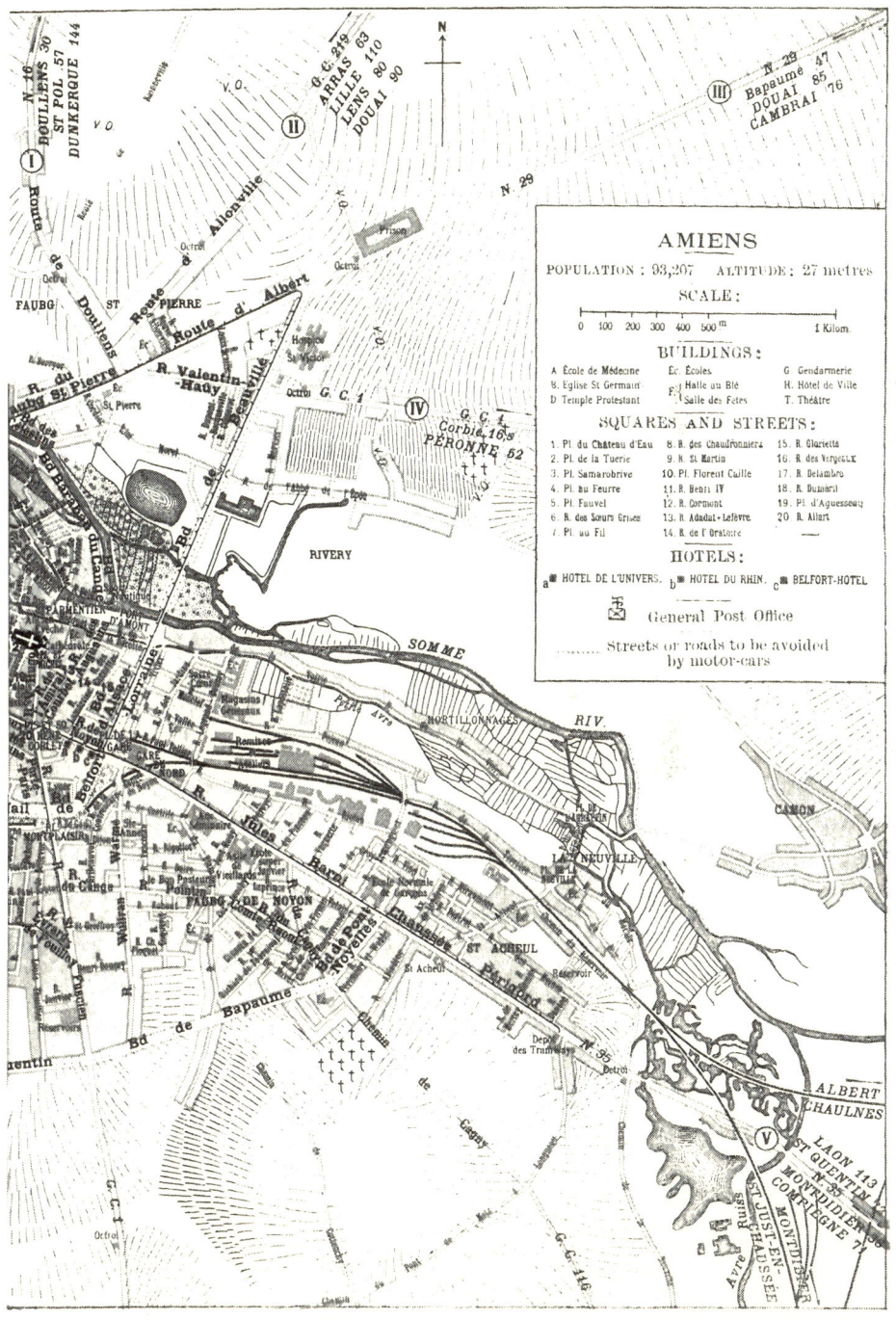

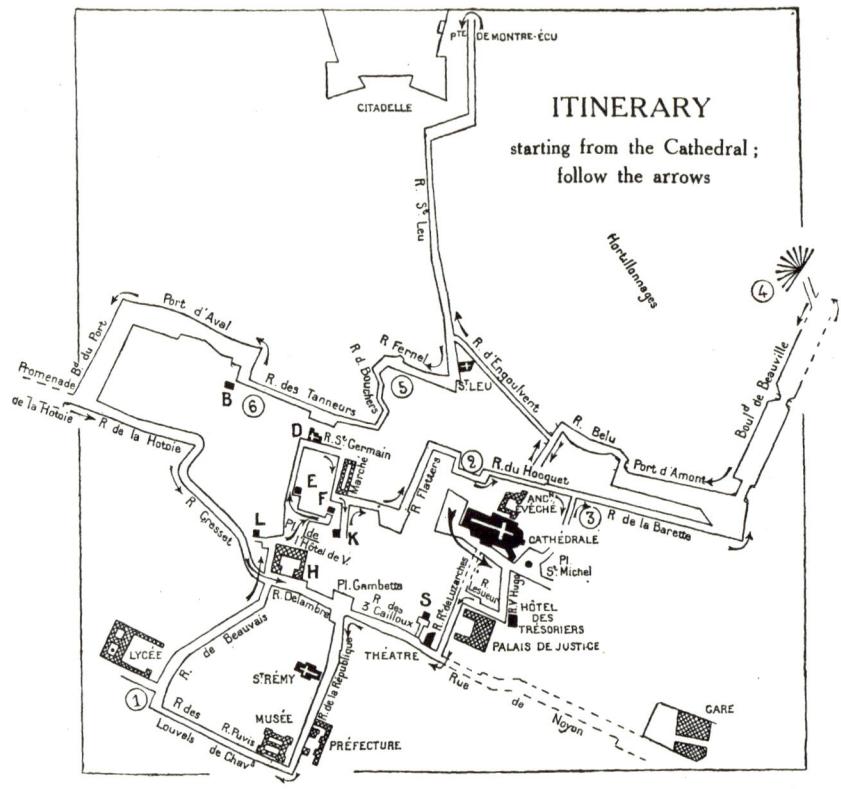

ITINERARY
starting from the Cathedral;
follow the arrows

EXPLANATION OF THE ARBITRARY SIGNS USED IN THE ITINERARY, AND THE CORRESPONDING PAGE-NUMBERS IN THE GUIDE.

The Cathedral, pp. 9-34.
U — Theatre, p. 35.
S — Logis du Gouverneur du Roi en Picardie, p. 36.
— Rue des Trois-Cailloux. p. 36.
— St. Rémy Church, p. 37.
— Museum, pp. 38-44.
— Prefecture, p. 45
1 — Corner of bombarded streets, p. 45.
H — Hôtel de Ville (Town Hall), p. 45.
L — Bailliage (Bailiwick), p. 46.
F — Maison du Blanc Pignon (House of the White Gable), p. 47.
E — Belfry, p. 47.
D — Church of St. Germain, pp. 47-48.
K — Maison du Sagittaire (Archers' House), p. 48.
2 — Place des Huchers, rue du Don and neighbouring streets, pp. 49-52
3 — Hocquet Canal, p. 50.
4 — Panorama of the Boulevard de Beauvillé, p. 50.
5 — Rue des Bouchers, p. 54.
6 — Rue des Tanneurs and Hôtel Morgan de Belloy, pp. 54-55.
B — Hôtel Morgan de Belloy, p.55.

ITINERARY

THE CATHEDRAL — VISIT TO THE TOWN

See opposite : Coloured plan, with detailed plan of centre of town and outline of itinerary at back.

What the Tourist should see

Do not omit : **The Cathedral** (*pp.* 9-36) especially the western and southern doorways, nave, stalls, and carving in the choir aisles.
Of great interest : PICARDY MUSEUM (*pp.* 40-45).
Archæological curiosities : FAÇADE OF THEATRE (*p.* 35), OLD HOUSES (*pp.* 47-56), CHURCHES OF ST. LEU (*pp.* 52-53), ST. GERMAIN (*pp.* 47-48) AND ST. RÉMY (*p.* 37).
Picturesque sights : ST. LEU QUARTER (*p.* 52), THE HORTILLONNAGES (*p.* 51).
Walks : HOTOIE PARK (*p.* 55), NEW BOULEVARDS, and THE RUE DE BEAUVAIS (*p.* 45), whose ruins attest the violence of the bombardment.
Specialities : Macaroons, potted duck.

Itinerary recommended for visiting Amiens

(*Distance :* 6½ *miles*)

Starting point : Place de la Cathédrale.

THE CATHEDRAL (*historical monument*)

The Cathedral at Amiens is the most perfect example of Gothic architecture extant, realizing as it does to the full, the possibilities of this style. According to Viollet-le-Duc, it is pre-eminently an " ogival church."
The Cathedral is typical, both from an architectural point of view, and also on account of its statues, which form one of the finest collections of Middle-Age sculpture. From an iconographic standpoint, this statuary constitutes one of the most complete summaries of the religious thought of past centuries.
The Cathedral (*see plan, p.* 22) covers a ground surface of about 9,000 square yards. Measured on the outside, it has a total length of about 480 feet and a width of 230 feet at the transept. It is the largest church in France.
The construction of the principal façade and nave was begun in 1220, from plans prepared by the architect, Robert de Luzarches, who was succeeded in his task by Thomas de Cormont and afterwards by his son, Renaud de Cormont.
Although no Cathedral has ever been built in entire conformity with the original plans, that of Amiens was probably completed more quickly than any other, and with less alteration of the original designs.
In 1269, fifty years after the commencement of the building operations, there only remained to be built the upper portion of the west façade and the two great rose-windows of the transept.
The only important alteration made in the original plans was the addition, in the 14th century, of chapels between the buttresses and flying-buttresses of the nave.
The Cathedral is built of grey limestone, on foundations 26 feet thick.

West Façade

The upper portion, consisting of two towers of unequal height, finished in different styles, belongs to the 14th century. The north tower, which is the higher, contains the great bells. The openings are decorated with statues of the Apostles, which have been either restored or renewed.

The upper storey of the south tower contains two bays with openings surmounted by gables. It is terminated by a pointed roof with a dormer-window and lead spikes. A gallery, called the ringers' gallery, with covered arcades surmounted by pinnacles and turrets, connects the two towers.

Below this gallery is the great rose-window, of which the frame-work

only belongs to the 13th century. The mullions are in the Flamboyant style. Below, running the whole length of the façade, are two superposed galleries.
The first contains twenty-two giant statues (over twelve feet high) of crowned kings bearing sceptres in their hands.
These statues have given rise to much controversy, some holding that they represent the kings of Judah, others, the kings of France.
The second gallery corresponds to the triforium in the interior.
Lastly, comes the great doorway (*photo below*) with its three large doors. On either side of the lateral doors are massive buttresses which gradually taper off, rising to the upper part of the façade.
On the front side of each are three statues of the lesser prophets, with their most notable prophecies carved in the quatre-foils of the bas-reliefs below.
The whole of the statuary of the great doorway dates back approximately to the period 1225-1235.

Central Doorway (*Door of St. Saviour*)

On the dividing pier: Statue of Christ, known as the " Beautiful God of Amiens" (*photos p.* 12).
Trampling the lion and dragon under-foot, he is blessing with his right hand, while in his left he holds a closed book.
On the socle are carved an asp and basilisk, symbolical of the " Evil One vanquished by Christ ! "
On the lower portion of the pillar is a crowned king, probably Solomon.
The two sides of the great doorway are similar in design.
(*a*) On the jambs of the door :
To the right of Christ are the five wise virgins bearing lamps full of oil in their hands. In the lower arcade, a vigorous tree represents the Bible bringing forth good fruit.

GREAT DOORWAY OF WEST FAÇADE (*Cliché LL*).

ST. FIRMIN'S DOOR   ST.-SAVIOUR'S DOOR   "MOTHER-OF-GOD" DOOR

"BEAUTIFUL GOD" STATUE ON DIVIDING PILLAR OF CENTRAL DOOR.

To the left of Christ are seen the five foolish virgins holding their lamps, reversed, while below is the " tree of evil " with withered trunk.

(b) On the piers of each splaying :
Six apostles and two of the greater prophets. These statues are nearly eight feet in height.

Nearly all the Apostles resemble Christ, having the same type of face (generally pronounced oval) and the same serene and noble expression.

On the basements, to the right and left :

1. Underneath the statues of the greater prophets four quatre-foils represent their principal prophecies.

2. Below the statues of the Apostles are twelve medallions in two rows. The upper one represents the six Virtues and the lower one the opposing Vices.

The Virtues are grave women seated, each with a shield bearing a distinctive emblem. On the other hand, the Vices are depicted by gesture.

The tympanum (*photo p.* 13) represents the complete story of the Last Judgment :

Lower portion : Above the lintel, which is decorated with a frieze of finely carved foliage, the resurrection is depicted. The dead, awakened by angels blowing trumpets, leave their graves. They are young, and either naked or scantily clothed.

In the centre St. Michael weighs the souls in a balance. In one of the scales is the Lamb of God which " taketh away the sins of the world," while in the other is the head of a demon.

Middle portion : Separation of the good from the evil.

To the left, the elect, clothed and serene, ascend to Heaven, where they are received by St. Peter ; to the right, a demon pushes the condemned into an enormous pair of open jaws representing the infernal regions.

HEAD OF THE "BEAUTIFUL GOD" STATUE.

Upper portion : Christ, surrounded by the Virgin and St. John kneeling, and by angels bearing the instruments of the Passion, judges mankind.

Above, in the point of the arch, the " Son of Man " half emerges from clouds, having in his mouth two swords. On either side is an angel, one bearing the sun, the other the moon, represented by discs.

The eight borders which form the arches on either side of the tympanum contain over 150 statues representing the celestial hierarchy.

In the lower row of the first six borders, scenes relating to the Last Judgment are also represented.

CENTRAL DOORWAY

TYMPANUM OF CENTRAL DOORWAY. (*page* 12) THE LAST JUDGMENT. (*Cliché LL*).

DETAILS OF CENTRAL PORCH (*left-hand side*)

CENTRAL PORCH (*left-hand side*).

The Apostles are represented in the following order (*from left to right*):

St. *Peter*, with cross and keys.

St. *Andrew*, with cross.

St. *James*, with sword (recalling his martyrdom), and wallet.

St. *John*, with beardless face, holds a cup, out of which comes a serpent.

The last two, with palm branch and axe, have not been identified.

The two prophets on the right are *Isaiah* (scroll) and *Jeremiah* (cross).

DIVIDING PILLAR OF "MOTHER-OF-GOD" DOOR WITH VIRGIN.

"MOTHER-OF-GOD" DOOR.

"Mother-of-God" door

(*See photo p.* 11)

This doorway has been dedicated to the Virgin, and forms one of the most complete representations of the worship of Mary produced by the iconographic statuary of the Middle Ages.

On the pier: A remarkably fine statue of the Virgin, belonging to the first half of the 13th century (*photo opposite*).

The six bas-reliefs of the pier basement represent the story of Adam and Eve: Creation of man — creation of woman —warning not to touch the forbidden fruit — the original sin — expulsion from the Garden of Eden — Adam and Eve at work.

On each side of the Virgin, in the splaying of the door, are six large statues :—

To the left : The Wise Men of the East offer presents to the child Jesus ; Herod questions the Wise Men ; Solomon and the Queen of Sheba.

To the right : Three groups of statues in pairs represent the Annunciation, Visitation, and Presentation (*photo below*).

From left to right :

1. Annunciation: Gabriel and Mary.

2. Visitation: Mary and Elizabeth.

3. Presentation : Virgin and Child and the High Priest Simeon.

The first two groups are especially remarkable for nobleness of attitude and harmonious robes.

On the basements, in the quatre-foil medallions, are carved various biblical scenes relating to the large statues surmounting them.

To the right, under the *Annunciation*, four medallions with figures of the Virgin according to the Mosaic Law : *The Stone rolling down from the Mountain ; Gideon's fleece.*

Below: *The Burning Bush ; Aaron's Rod.*

Under the *Visitation : The Nativity of St. John the Baptist ; Annunciation of the coming birth of John, to Zachariah ; Zachariah struck*

"MOTHER-OF-GOD" DOOR

dumb for unbelief. Below: *Birth of St. John* and *Zachariah naming the child John.*

Under the *Presentation* are four scenes from the childhood of Christ: *Flight into Egypt ; Falling down of the Egyptian Idols at the approach of Jesus.* Below: *Jesus in the midst of the Doctors ; Jesus taken back to Nazareth* (*photo p.* 14).

To the left, under *The Wise Men and Herod,* story of the Wise Men: *Balaam's star ; Micah's prophecy at Bethlehem ; The Wise Men before Herod ; Massacre of the Innocents.* Below: *The Wise Men warned in a dream to return by another way ; the Wise Men depart by ship fr m Tharsis ; Burning of the Fleet of Tharsis ; Herod orders the ships of Tharsis to be burnt.*

Under *Solomon and the Queen of Sheba ; Solomon receives the Queen of Sheba ; Solomon on his throne ; Solomon's feast.* Below: *Solomon praying ; Solomon shows his treasures to the Queen of Sheba.*

The tympanum (*photo below*) is divided into three parts:

1. Six patriarchs or prophets.

2. *Left :* Burial of the Virgin. *Right :* The Assumption.

3. Crowning of the Virgin.

In the arches are angels bearing censers, the Kings of Judah and other ancestors of the Virgin.

TYMPANUM OF THE "MOTHER-OF-GOD" DOOR.

St. Firmin's door (see p. 11)

This door was dedicated to the religious history of Picardy. A fine statue of St. Firmin, first bishop of Amiens, adorns the dividing pier. Crosier in hand and mitre on head, he blesses the faithful (*photo below*).

ST. FIRMIN'S DOOR.

Left: St Firmin blessing.   *Right:* 6 statues of bishops and martyrs.   *In medallions:* Peasants' calendar (*December-May*) with zodiacal signs.

On either side are six large statues representing the most notable among the first bishops, martyrs, and saints of the diocese (*photo above*).

Scenes illustrating the round of tasks of the peasants are carved in the medallions on the basement. Above each scene of digging, reaping, harvesting, etc., appears the zodiacal sign of the corresponding month.

In the calendar of Amiens, the year opens with the month of December and the sign of Capricorn (*first medallion on the right*).

The reading of the calendar should begin there (*photo above*).

December.   The peasant kills his pig for the feasts at the end of the year.
January.   He is seated at a well supplied table.
February.   He warms himself at the fire.
March.   Work begins again in the fields ; tilling the soil.
April.   Pruning the vines
May.   The peasant rests before the labours of Summer.

The calendar terminates on the left-hand side of the basement.
The tympanum (*photo p.* 17) depicts the history of the relics of St. Firmin :
1st portion : Six bishops seated.
2nd portion : Discovery of the body of St. Firmin by the bishop St. Sauve.
3rd portion : Solemn translation of the relics.
Statues of angels appear on the borders of the arches.

TYMPANUM OF
ST. FIRMIN'S
DOOR.
—
LIFE OF
ST. FIRMIN.

South Lateral Façade

At the foot of the south tower is St. Christopher's door (*plan p. 22*), and to the right a statue of this saint carrying the child Jesus on his shoulder.

The buttresses separating the lofty, broad windows of the chapels of the nave, added in the 14th century, are decorated with superposed statues.

The gable of the south transept (*photo opposite*) is remarkable.

The upper portion of the great rose window is surrounded by a " wheel of fortune " (14th century).

On one side eight beardless youths climb up the wheel, while on the other side eight old men with beards descend with it.

In the middle is seated a figure with crown and sceptre.

GABLE OF
SOUTH
TRANSEPT.
(*facing the Rue Robert de Luzarches*).

SOUTH LATERAL FAÇADE

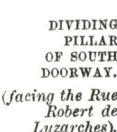

DIVIDING PILLAR OF SOUTH DOORWAY.
(*facing the Rue Robert de Luzarches*).

THE "GILDED VIRGIN"

Doorway of the South Transept

(" *Gilded Virgin* " *Door*)

This door was dedicated to the saints of Picardy, but especially to St. Honoré, who was one of the first bishops of Amiens. It is also sometimes called the St. Honoré Door.

The statuary dates back to the end of the 13th century, with the exception of the large statues on the jambs, which were executed at the time the doorway was built, *i.e.*, about 1230. These eight statues represent six saints and two angels.

On the dividing pillar is the celebrated statue of the Gilded Virgin (*photo above*) standing with the Child Jesus on her left arm, on which side the hip slightly protrudes. It is one of the earliest examples of this *irregularity of outline*, and was destined to inspire the Virgins of the 14th and 15th centuries, in which this characteristic became increasingly marked.

A comparison of this statue with that of the south door of the west façade (*photo p.* 14), furnishes a striking example of the evolution which statuary had undergone in three-quarters of a century. The Gilded Virgin (end of 13th century) is represented as a gracious young mother tenderly regarding her child, while the " Mother-of-God " gravely bears the " King of the World."

On the tympanum (*photo p.* 19) are:

(*a*) On the lintel: Twelve exceedingly fine, 13th century statues of the Apostles.

The latter converse with animation in pairs. The expression of their faces is quite different from that of the Apostles on the central doorway, the appearance of the latter being solemn and almost godlike (*photo p.* 13).

(*b*) The upper four sections represent the life of St. Honoré:

1ST SECTION:

To the left, consecration of St. Honoré;
To the right, the voice of Lupicin reveals the shrines of the martyrs.

2ND SECTION:

To the left, St. Honoré celebrating mass; a divine hand blesses the elements;
To the right, the blind receive their sight.

DOORWAY OF SOUTH TRANSEPT

SOUTH
DOORWAY.
(*facing the
Rue Robert
de Luzarches*).

ON DIVIDING
PILLAR,
"GILDED
VIRGIN."

3RD SECTION :
Procession bearing the remains of St. Honoré.

4TH SECTION :
A crucifix, between the Virgin and St. John, reminds the faithful that the crucifix of a church, before which the procession passed, bowed its head as the remains of St. Honoré were carried by.

The arches comprise four borders with statues representing angels with crowns or censers, the sixteen patriarchs of the Mosaic law, the sixteen prophets and, lastly, sixteen figures of Apostles, evangelists, and holy women.

APSE
(Cliché LL.)

The Apse (photo above)

Built after the nave in 1240-1269, the apse is especially remarkable for the elegance and simplicity of its lines.

At the end are seven chapels, the central one being much deeper than the others. All are of open construction, the lofty windows being separated by heavily projecting buttresses. These chapels are noteworthy for their harmonious proportions and purity of style.

The distance to be spanned by the flying buttresses being too great, the latter were made in two parts, equipoised on an intermediate tambour; and whereas this arch, which is hollowed out by a series of small openwork ornamental arcades, is single in the lower flight, it became necessary, in the 15th century, to strengthen the upper flight below the arcades, with a second arch, on account of the pressure from the vaults.

Abutting on the south side of the apse is the Chapel of the Maccabees, so called because it formerly adjoined the cloister of the Cathedral, on whose walls was painted the Dance of Death. It now serves as a vestry.

The octagonal spire which rises above the intersection of the transept should be viewed from behind the apse.

It was built in 1529-1533 of horse-chestnut wood covered with thick sheet lead. 350 feet in height, it is only supported by four massive pillars at the intersection of the transept. The lower portion comprises two storeys of open construction ornamented with tall lead statues of saints.

North Lateral Façade

The doorway of the northern arm of the transept, also known as the door of St. Firmin the Confessor, is of the same construction as that of the southern arm, but is unadorned with sculpture. The dividing pillar alone is ornamented with a 13th century statue of a bishop.

In the tympanum is a glazed, packed wall which dates from the beginning of the 14th century; the nerves represent an enormous spider.

The upper portion is unfinished; the rose window is bare of any orna-

mentation, and there is no stone gable.

As in the case of the south façade, the chapels of the nave are separated on the outside by buttresses ornamented with 14th century statues.

The two chapels nearest the principal façade were the last to be built (1373-1375), and it was Jean de la Grange, then Bishop of Amiens, and afterwards Cardinal and Financial Comptroller to Charles V., who bore the expense of the building. A massive buttress was built to strengthen the north tower, which these later constructions had weakened.

Two of the sides of the buttress and the dividing pillar between the two chapels are ornamented with three superposed statues of considerable interest, both from an historical and artistic point of view.

Considered downwards they represent :

STATUES ON NORTH TOWER BUTTRESS :
(on left) CHARLES V.
(on right) THE DAUPHIN.

On the north side of the buttress : *St. John the Baptist, the Dauphin Charles (later Charles VI.—photo above)* and *Bureau de la Rivière*, Counsellor to Charles V. and VI.

On the west side of the buttress : *The Virgin, King Charles V. (photo above)*, and *Cardinal Jean de la Grange*.

On the dividing pillar between the two chapels : *St. Firmin the Confessor, Louis of Orleans (second son of Charles V.) and a Counsellor of the King.*

Flying Buttresses

(photo opposite)

The flying buttresses of the nave are characteristic of the great Gothic period.

Built of massive masonry, each consists of two superposed arches, one above and the other below the point of abutment of the ogival arches of the great nave.

These flying buttresses provide a counter-thrust which partly annuls that of the vault.

The remainder is taken by the massive buttresses surmounted by pinnacles and turrets, the latter preventing them from giving way under the continual thrust of the flying-buttresses.

FLYING BUTTRESSES OF NAVE WITH TWO SUPERPOSED ARCHES. (Cliché LL.)

PLAN OF CATHEDRAL.

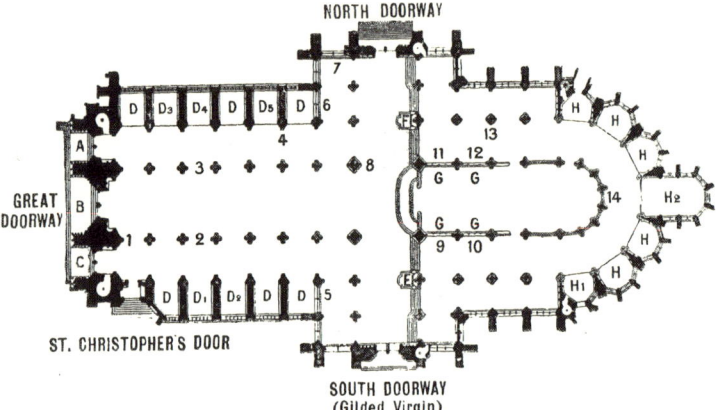

KEY TO PLAN OF AMIENS CATHEDRAL

A. Great doorway ; St. Firmin's Door.
B.   ,,   ,,   ; St. Saviour's Door,
C.   ,,   ,,   ; " Mother of God Door."
D. Chapels of the nave (14th century).
D1. Chapel of the Annunciation or Our Lady of Faith (Annunciation by *Blasset*).
D2- Chapel of the Assumption (Assumption by *Blasset*).
D3.   ,,   ,,   Our Lady of Help (altar screen by *Blasset*).
D4.   ,,   ,,   St. Saviour (ancient crucifix).
D5.   ,,   ,,   Our Lady of Peace (Virgin and child by *Blasset*).
E. Altar of Our Lady of Puy (1627-1623) by *Blasset* (on altar screen : painting of Assumption by *Francken*).
F. Altar of St. Sebastian (1634-1635), by *Blasset*.
G. Stalls.
H. Radiating chapels of the apse.
H1. Chapel of St. Eloi (The Prophetesses, pai :tings, 1506).
H2.   ,,   ,,   the Virgin.
1. Tomb of Canon Pierre Burry (16th century).
2. Bronze tomb to Evrard de Fouilloy (13th century).
3.   ,,   ,,   ,,   Geoffroy d'Eu (13th century).
4. Monument to Jean de Sachy, by *Blasset* (17th century).
5. Life of St. James the Less (stone carving, 16th century).
6. Jesus driving the buyers and sellers out of the Temple (stone carving, 16th century).
7. Roman cistern (12th century).
8. Tomb of Cardinal Hémard de Denouville (1543).
9. Life of St. Firmin, enclosure of carved stone, painted and gilded (end of 15th century), and funeral statue of Feray de Beauvoir with 16th century paintings.
10. Continuation of the Life of St. Firmin, stone enclosure and tomb of Adrien de Henencourt (16th century).
11-12. Life of St. John the Baptist, stone enclosure (1531).
13. Mausoleum of Ant. de Ballon, by *Blasset* (17th century).
14. Recumbent statue of Cardinal Jean de la Grange (15th century) and tomb of Canon Guilain Lucas with Weeping Angel statue, by *Blasset* (17th century).

Interior of Cathedral

The Cathedral has an inside overall length of nearly 440 feet and a breadth of about 200 feet in the transept.

It comprises : The great nave, composed of six bays with aisles and posterior chapels (14th century).

The transept with aisle and three bays in each arm.

The choir, composed of four bays and double aisle.

The seven-sided apsis with ambulatory, on which open out seven pentagonal radiating chapels.

The most striking features of the interior are its great height, the few points of support, and the simple character of the latter.

The Great Nave

(*photo opposite*)

GREAT NAVE.
(*height* 140 *ft.*)
(*Cliché LL.*)

The great nave, which is about 48 feet wide, is nearly 140 feet high, and is the second highest Gothic vault in France (that of the choir of Beauvais Cathedral is about 156 feet high).

Few edifices exist in which the solid parts have been so reduced in favour of the spaces.

There are no walls; the cathedral may be said to consist of windows, rose-windows, and " stone lace-work."

The strength of the whole structure depends upon a series of pillars and arches which, according to the principles of Gothic construction, ensure equilibrium, by dividing the pressures and opposing conflicting stresses.

The triforium has lost that importance which it had in the early Gothic edifices. Here it is a narrow gallery running right round the church. In the nave it comprises, at each bay, two wide arches divided by two slender columns.

The windows are 52 feet high and of the same width as the arcades on the ground floor.

The original stained glass no longer exists.

According to the canons of Gothic art, all ornamental carving must be inspired by Nature.

The typical ornamentation for capitals is the crocket, intermingled here and there with other kinds of foliage.

The belt of foliage below the triforium represents plants grown exclusively in Picardy, and is very finely executed.

At the entrance to the nave, with its back to the first pillar on the right, is the early 16th century tomb of Canon Pierre Burry (1 *on plan*). It is a fine, expressive statue of the canon kneeling, presented by his Patron Saint, St. Peter, to an " Ecce Homo " of little note.

TOMB OF
EVRARD
DE FOUILLOY.
(2 on plan).

On each side of the great nave, below the longitudinal arcades and between the second and third pillars, are two bronze tombs supported by lions. These are the tombs of the two bishops who founded the Cathedral, and who are represented on large rectangular tablets, wearing chasuble and mitre. Beautifully executed, they are practically the only remaining specimens in France of early funeral sculpture.

To the left, is the tomb of Geoffroy d'Eu, deceased in 1230 (3 on plan).

To the right (2 on plan): that of Evrard de Fouilloy, who died in 1222 (photo opposite).

The pulpit of painted and gilded wood belongs to the end of the 18th century. It backs up against one of the northern pillars and is carried by three tall statues representing the virtues : Faith, Hope, and Charity.

The Aisles

The aisles are extremely lofty, the keystones of the vaults being richly sculptured.

Chapels added in the 14th century terminate the aisles.

Nearly all contain works of art by a local sculptor very well known in Picardy : *Nicolas Blasset* (1600-1659).

The following are of especial interest :

I. **South Aisle :**

Third chapel (Annunciation—*D* 1 *on plan*) ; on the altar, bas-relief by *Blasset*, representing *The Annunciation* ;

Fourth chapel (Assumption—*D* 2 *on plan*) ; on the altar, fine Virgin by *Blasset* (*The Assumption*).

II. **North Aisle :**

Second chapel (Our Lady of Help—*D* 3 *on plan*) ; on the altar screen, *Virgin and child trampling on serpent representing Death* (*Blasset*) ;

Third chapel (St. Saviour's—*D* 4 *on plan*) : tall Byzantine Christ of wood known as " St. Saviour " ;

Fifth chapel (Our Lady of Peace—*D* 5 *on plan*) : *Virgin* by *Blasset*.

Against the pillar which separates the fifth and sixth chapels is the funeral monument of *Jean de Sachy*, Sheriff of Amiens, and his wife, one of *Blasset's* finest masterpieces. Both the deceased are represented kneeling before the Virgin, to whom they are made known by John the Baptist.

The Transept (*photo p. 25*)

At the intersection of the transept, four massive pillars composed of sixteen columns rise up to the vault.

There is a fine rose-window at each end. That of the south arm, with curved mullions, is in the Flamboyant style, and contains portions of the original stained glass (*see heads of angels*).

That in the north arm (*photo p. 25*) belongs to the 14th century. Part of the original stained glass still exists, though restored.

Under each rose window are two superposed, open-work galleries containing fragments of old stained glass representing persons.

Two altars of similar design by *Blasset* were erected between 1625 and 1635, one in each arm, forming pendants.

Four tall statues, two seated and two standing, form the framework of an altar-screen with painting, the latter surmounted by the statue of the patron of the chapel.

The altar of the south arm (*E on plan*) is dedicated to *Our Lady of Puy*, representing drawing a child out of a well (*photo opposite.*)

The painting of the altar-screen by the Flemish artist François Francken (*The Assumption*), is the finest in the Cathedral.

THE TRANSEPT, NORTH ARM.
(*to the right*): THE CHOIR.
(*in foreground*): ALTAR OF OUR LADY OF PUY.

The altar in the north arm (*F on plan*) is dedicated to *St. Sebastian*, seen at the top pierced with arrows.

In the aisle of each arm, against the enclosure wall of the last chapel in the nave, will be seen in Flamboyant style niches, early 16th century carvings representing : *In the south arm*, an episode in the life of St. James the Less (5 *on plan*), and *in the north arm* (6 *on plan*), the story of Jesus driving the buyers and sellers out of the Temple (*photo p. 26*).

These carvings have never been restored.

Other noteworthy objects in the transept are :

1. *South arm :* In the arcading of the Gilded Virgin Door are three fine late 13th century statues of angels with the instruments of the Passion. At the top of the pediment is a statue of St. Michael (16th century).

Below the stone carvings in the aisles, *eight black marble tables*, surmounted by small *bas-reliefs* by *Blasset* representing the principal episodes in the life of the Virgin.

On the tables are inscribed all the names, with their respective devices, of the *Masters of the Brotherhood of our Lady of Puy*, from 1389 to 1729 (*p. 42*)

North arm (*photo above*): Stone and white marble tomb of Cardinal Hémard de Denouville (8 *on plan*), fine Renaissance monument (1543) backed up against one of the pillars at the intersection of the transept.

The statues of the four cardinal virtues, carved in demi-relief in the arcades of the basement, are especially worthy of notice. They are shown

CHOIR AND APSE

JESUS DRIVING THE BUYERS AND SELLERS OUT OF THE TEMPLE.

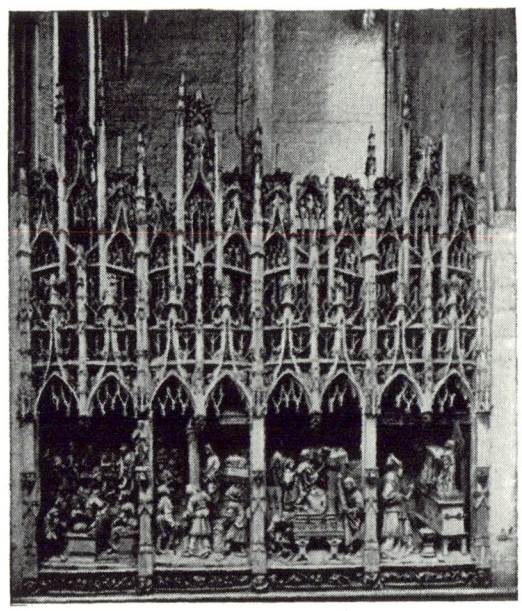

*In each niche, part of the Temple at Jerusalem is represented.
In the two left-hand sections: Jesus and the buyers and sellers in the atrium and The Tabernacle.
In the other two sections: The Temple proper (Sanctuary and Holy of Holies).*

holding their traditional attributes, and represent (*from left to right*): *Justice*, with sword and scales; *Temperance*, with clock; *Prudence*, with clock and compasses; *Force*, with tower, out of which comes a monster.

In a niche, above this basement, is the Cardinal kneeling before the head of St. John the Baptist. On the crown are three small statues representing the virtues: Faith, Hope and Charity. At the end of the aisle is a curious, late 12th century *Roman cistern* (7 *on plan*) ornamented at the corners with the statues of four prophets.

Choir and Apse

Fine wrought-iron railings were placed, in the 18th century, at the principal and side entrances to the choir, as also between the columns enclosing the chancel. Contrary to the practice usually observed till then in Gothic edifices, in which building generally began with the choir, this part of the Cathedral was built after the nave.

The later period of construction is most noticeable in the triforium, which has not the simple elegance of the nave.

The arrangement of the bays is entirely different, the latter being surmounted by a gable decorated with crockets, while the end wall is of open construction.

Remains of 13th century stained glass are still to be seen in the triforium and the great window in the centre of the apse. The latter, dating from 1269, is practically intact.

Behind the high altar, an 18th century "glory," representing angels and cherubs, interrupts the view of the interior of the Cathedral.

CHOIR
STALLS
(Cliché LL)

Choir Stalls

The stalls (*G on plan*) are of oak and were made by the wood-cutters and wood-carvers of Amiens (1508–1519). They are in the Gothic-Flamboyant style, with Renaissance architectural and ornamental motifs.

It is impossible to praise too highly the perfection of even the smallest details of this woodwork, which is unrivalled throughout France. Especially worthy of remark is the consummate skill with which the joints have been concealed in the assembling.

To-day, 110 in number, the stalls extend the entire length of the choir aisles in a double row: high stalls and low stalls.

The high stalls, with very elevated backs simply decorated with an arch in accolade, are covered by a continuous canopy ornamented with pinnacles and pendentives of the finest workmanship.

To the right and left of the entrance to the choir, two larger stalls with separate canopies are surmounted by a pyramid fifty-three feet high, carrying the statues of the Church and Synagogue.

These are the master-stalls.

The two terminal stalls near the chancel are likewise surmounted by a pyramid with small statues.

Both as regards woodwork and carving, the stalls are rightly considered masterpieces, in the latter respect, on account of the infinite variety of

DETAILS
OF STALLS;
COMPASSION
SEAT
REPRESENTING
ABRAHAM
SACRIFICING
ISAAC.

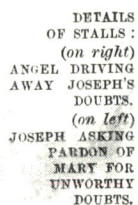

DETAILS
OF STALLS :
(on right)
ANGEL DRIVING
AWAY JOSEPH'S
DOUBTS.
(on left)
JOSEPH ASKING
PARDON OF
MARY FOR
UNWORTHY
DOUBTS.

subjects, profusion of figures and extreme delicacy of ornamentation. The finish and detail are truly extraordinary.

The scenes represented belong to two different classes :

1. On the stalls proper, including the seats, but excepting the elbow or hand-rests, and on the hand-rails and panels of the passages leading from the low stalls to the high stalls, are represented the *Story of the Creation* from Adam to Job, and the *Life of the Virgin*.

2. On the elbow-rests of the stalls and—alternated with clusters of leaves —on the pendentives of the canopy, subjects taken from the lives of the burgesses and artisans at the beginning of the 16th century (especially the handicrafts then practised), fables (*the Fox preaching to the Hens*) and satirical or fanciful scenes are depicted.

In the biblical and other subjects dealt with, the buildings, costumes, insides of houses, furniture and various accessories belong to the time when they were carved. Consequently, in addition to their artistic value, the stalls form an historical document of great value.

DETAILS
OF STALLS :
ELBOW-REST
REPRESENTING
APOTHECARY
COMPOUNDING
DRUGS.

Chapels in Apse

The seven radial chapels of the apse are pentagonal, the central one having two bays more than the others.

Starting at the south aisle, the first chapel (*St. Eloi*—*H* 1 *on plan*) is decorated on the basement of the two west bays, with eight fine though greatly deteriorated figures of prophetesses (1506).

The third, fourth, and fifth chapels were restored by *Viollet-le-Duc*, in the 19th century, in accordance with the decorative scheme employed in the 13th century.

The fourth chapel (that of the *Virgin*—*H* 2 *on plan*) contains some 13th century restored stained glass (scenes from the *Life of the Virgin and Tree of Jesse*).

On the left, let into the sides of the wall, are two 14th century tombstones.

The basement carrying the two recumbent statues is ornamented with arcading and mourners, this being one of the earliest examples of that type of decoration, since so frequently uesd for funeral monuments.

TOMB OF CANON GUILAIN LUCAS WITH " WEEPING ANGEL" STATUE.

Opposite the chapel of the Virgin, with its back to the intercolumniation of the chancel, is the *mausoleum of Canon Guilain Lucas* (*photo opposite and 14 on plan*)—benefactor of orphans and children in the 17th century—*Blasset's* most celebrated but not finest masterpiece. The Canon is shown kneeling before the Virgin, while between the two statues is a cherub known as " The Weeping Angel " (*photo above*).

Below the mausoleum is a white marble statue of *Cardinal Jean de la Grange*, deceased in 1402.

Choir Aisles

The enclosure walls of the first two bays of the north and south choir aisles are covered with stone carving dating from 1489-1530.

Each bay comprises four large Gothic-Flamboyant niches containing the same number of carved groups. A versified legend in French accompanies each subject treated. Below, is a lofty basement almost entirely covered with carved medallions.

The stone sculpture which decorates the northern enclosure of the choir depicts eight scenes from the life of St. John the Baptist.

(a) *In the first bay coming from the apse* (12 *on plan*):—

Vengeance of Herod's wife. — Beheading of St. John the Baptist. — Herod's feast. — Imprisonment of St. John the Baptist.

(b) *In the second bay* (*that nearest the transept*—11 *on plan*) :—

St. John showing the Lamb of God. — St. John revealing his mission

CHOIR
AISLES.
(9 on plan)
LIFE OF
ST. FIRMIN.

to Herod's messengers. — Baptism of Christ. — St. John preaching in the wilderness.

The very fine medallions on the basement complete the story of the saint.

The **mausoleum** (by *Blasset*) of Canon Antoine de Baillon backs up against one of the pillars of the first of the two bays. He is shown kneeling before Ecce Homo (13 *on plan*). It will be noticed that the features of this Christ recall those of the Louis XIV. period, and in no way resemble the face usually attributed to Christ in the Middle Ages.

The finest sculpture is in the south aisle.

The first bay (9 *on plan*—*photo p.* 30) portrays in four main scenes the life of St. Firmin.

These are (*from the left to right*) :—
1. Arrival of the saint at Amiens.
2. Preaching the Gospel to the inhabitants.
3. Baptising the people of Amiens.
4. Arrest and decapitation.

At the back of the four niches, a **panoramic view** has been painted of Amiens, as it was at the end of the 15th century. Judging from the perspective of the Cathedral, which appears in the fourth group, this painting is very true to life.

To the right and left of the carvings are **statues** of the donor, Adrien de Henencourt, and St. Firmin.

In the centre of the basement, in a niche at the bottom of which is a **painting** of the twelve Apostles, a reclining **statue** of Ferry de Beauvoir, Bishop of Amiens, should be noticed. On each side there are remarkable **paintings** of two angels lifting a red cloth, and two canons with cope and cassock holding a pall decorated with the figure of Agnus Dei and the symbols of the four Evangelists.

The whole dates from about 1489. The carvings are the oldest of all those in the aisles, and are distinguishable from the others by the

CHOIR AISLES. (10 on plan) REVELATION AND TRANSLATION OF REMAINS OF ST. FIRMIN.

garments, which fall in long, straight, stiff folds, and their greater simplicity.

The second bay (10 *on plan, photo p.* 31) recalls the legend of the discovery and translation of the remains of St. Firmin.

From left to right :—
1. St. Sauve, Bishop of Amiens, exhorting the faithful to pray, that the sepulchre of the saint might be revealed.
2. Ray of light revealing the sepulchre to St. Sauve during Mass.
3. Exhuming the body .
4. Translating the remains of St. Firmin to Amiens.

The basement comprises thirteen carved **medallions** illustrating various episodes in the life of St. Firmin, while in the middle is seen an exceedingly fine recumbent **statue** of Adrien de Henencourt, dean of the chapter of Amiens, who died in 1530, and at whose expense the whole of the south enclosure of the choir was built.

CATHEDRAL TREASURE (*in Vestry*) : ST. FIRMIN'S SHRINE.

PROTECTION
OF DOORWAYS
OF PRINCIPAL
FAÇADE,

THE CATHEDRAL DURING THE WAR

During the **War,** elaborate precautions were taken to protect the Cathedral and its art treasures from the dangers of bombardment. The three doorways of the principal façade (*photo above*) and that of the Gilded Virgin, were covered with a thick protecting wall of sandbags.

The choir stalls (*photo p.* 33) were enclosed with reinforced concrete and sandbags, the stone carvings of the ambulatory being protected in like manner. The various funeral monuments were walled in, while firemen from Paris removed the stained glass. All the movable art treasures were taken away and placed in safety (*photo p.* 33).

CHAPEL OF
ST. JOHN
THE BAPTIST
DAMAGED
BY SHELL
(*left-hand
side of Apse*).

PROTECTION OF THE CHOIR STALLS.

These precautions were not superfluous, as the cathedral was repeatedly made the target of enemy artillery fire. In 1915, during an air bombardment, three out of nine bombs fell in the immediate vicinity, at distances varying from 150 to 200 yards. In the spring of 1918 an incendiary shell burst in the Rue de Robert Luzarches, within 30 yards of the Virgin doorway, completely destroying two houses, while splinters hit the upper part of the doorway above the wall of sandbags. In all, nine shells hit the cathedral, but none of them caused very serious damage.

The roof was pierced in several places, particularly on the south side of the choir, and the vault was perforated in the south aisle of the choir and in the nave. The gallery of the triforium was likewise torn open on the south side of the nave, while the chapels of St. John the Baptist (*photo* p. 32) and Our Lady of Faith (D 1 *on plan*) were damaged. Outside, the façades were struck with shell splinters, while here and there buttresses, flying-buttresses, and mullions of windows were broken or damaged.

(*See outline opposite p. 9 and plan opposite p. 8*).

On leaving the Cathedral by the

TAKING DOWN THE STATUES IN TRANSEPT.

EFFECT OF FIRST SHELLS WHICH HIT THE CATHEDRAL. ASPECT INSIDE THE NAVE.

CHIMERICAL FIGURES AND GARGOYLES
(*Cliché LL.*)

GENERAL VIEW OF THE CATHEDRAL. (*seen from the Hôtel de Ville*).

doorway of the south transept (Gilded Virgin Door), the tourist should skirt the Cathedral on the left as far as the Place St. Michel, which is behind the Apsis. In the middle of the Square is a **statue** *to Peter the Hermit. On the right of the Square, take the Rue Victor Hugo.*

At No. 36, hidden from the road by a high enclosure wall, is the very handsome brick and stone bossage **façade** (1634) of what were formerly the offices of the French Treasury. A bomb damaged the right-hand corner of the roof.

Turn into the first street on the right (Rue Lesueur), which skirts the Palais de Justice. *Turn to the left into the Rue de Robert de Luzarches, which passes in front of the principal façade of the* Palais de Justice (plan). Built towards the end of the 19th century, it contains some fine **woodwork** by Crescent.

Follow the Rue de Luzarches to the Rue des Trois-Cailloux ; on turning to the right, the tourist passes in front of the **Theatre.**

A large opening was made by a shell in the left-hand upper portion of the **façade** (*photo below*), which is pure Louis XVI in style.

This façade was built in 1778-1780.

It is remarkable for its harmonious proportions, as also for the delicacy and sobriety of its ornamentation.

The corner **pilasters** are decorated with lyres, surmounted by flaming tripods.

The central **pilasters** are ornamented with two groups of Muses in relief, one representing Dancing and Music, the other Comedy and Tragedy.

On the upper portion of each pilaster, the attributes of the four Muses have been carved in oval **medallions.**

THE THEATRE.

RUE DES TROIS-CAILLOUX

(*Photo taken from the Place Gambetta, April* 24th, 1918)

The interior of the theatre is interesting, by reason of the date of its construction (1773-1779). It is the oldest playhouse in France.

Opposite the theatre, the shops of the **Nouvelles Galeries** were entirely destroyed (*photo below*).

At No. 59, *Rue des Trois-Cailloux, to the left of the theatre, is the Passage du Logis du Roi, where are to be found the remains of the* **" Logis du Gouverneur du Roi de Picardie "** (*House of the King of Picardy's Governor, S on outline of tour*).

Built about 1520 of brick and stone, the castle was mutilated in the 18th century. The outbuildings now serve various foreign purposes, and include a café, so that the place has lost most of its interest.

Only the **donjon tower,** from which there is a fine view over the whole city, retains its ancient aspect.

Follow the Rue des Trois - Cailloux to the Place Gambetta, then turn to the left into the Rue de la République, where, on the right, will be found :

RUE DES TROIS-CAILLOUX NEAR THE PLACE GAMBETTA

(" Magasins des Nouvelles Galeries," burnt on June 9th, 1918)

THE CHURCH OF ST. RÉMY

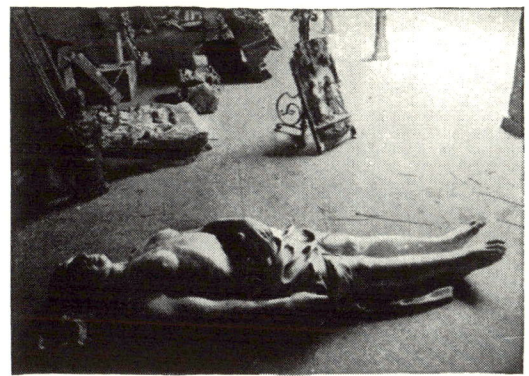

BROKEN STATUE OF MADELEINE DE MUTTEREL
(*Tomb of Nicolas de Lannoy, St. Rémy's Church, p 37*)

The Church of St. Rémy, which is being rebuilt on the site of the old church of the Couvent des Cordeliers (*Convent of the Franciscans or Grey Friars*).

It contains several pieces of **sculpture** by *Blasset*, including the monumental **tomb** of Nicholas de Lannoy, High Constable of Bourbonnais, and Madeleine de Mutterel, his wife, with their **statues** (1631)—*photos on this page*—and a **Virgin** known as the Condé Virgin, because it was given by the Prince of Condé after his victory at Rocroi.

A bomb caused nearly all the roof to fall in and seriously damaged the stained glass windows.

A little further on, on the same side of the street, is the **Museum.**

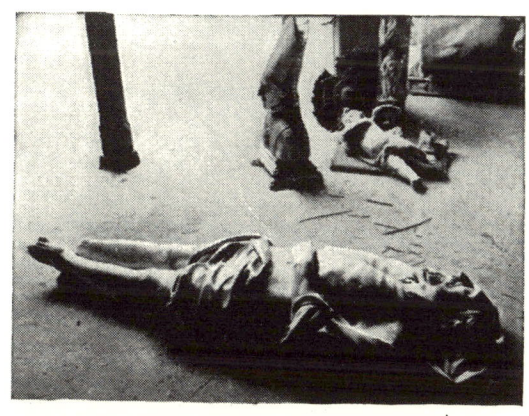

BROKEN STATUE OF NICOLAS DE LANNOY
(*Tomb in St. Rémy's Church, p. 37*)

MUSEUM: RIGHT WING OF REAR FAÇADE DAMAGED BY AERIAL TORPEDO IN 1918.

THE PICARDY MUSEUM

The Museum is installed in a spacious building erected in the middle of the 19th century at the expense of the Society of Antiquaries of Picardy, and afterwards handed over by it to the City. Most of the collections had fortunately been removed to a place of safety before the bombardment of 1918, which damaged the building. Three aerial torpedoes fell on the right wing of the rear façade (*photo above*), considerably damaging the collection of drawings by the brothers Duthoit.

The Museum will only be re-installed after the necessary repairs have been done, and as new classifications may then be made, the principal works of art are here dealt with according to category and date, instead of room by room.

A.- Sculpture

I.—*Greek and Gallo-Roman Antiquities.*

Triple Hecate: Grecian marble, very finely executed, representing the three divinities of the lunar month : Diana, Artemicia, and Hecate.

Gallo-Roman funeral stele with galloping cavalier carved in demi-relief.

Carved tombstone representing the deceased, holding lamp and purse, between two relations.

II.—*Middle Age and Renaissance Sculpture.*

Quadrangular baptismal font in pure Roman style.

Very fine late 12th century capitals, taken from the ancient monastery of the Premonstrants of Dommartin (Pas-de-Calais).

Tomb of black Tournai stone, belonging to the first half of the 15th century, representing *Knight Robert de Bouberch* in armour.

Very fine late 15th century Virgin of wood, painted and gilded, taken from the ancient church of the Minimes d'Amiens.

A series of merry monks' heads with caricatured features, carved in oak at the end of the 15th century ; very curious ; were formerly corbels supporting the framework of a house in Amiens.

III.—*Modern Sculpture.*

Puget, rough model in terra-cotta, used for the " Hercule gaulois " in the Louvre.

Coysevox, very fine marble bust of Regent Philip of Orléans. The wig is noteworthy, by reason of the exceeding delicacy of execution. Also bust of Chauvelin, intendant of Picardy.

Falguières, bronze bust of Gambetta, particularly expressive,

B.—Painting.

The museum of paintings includes :

I.—A series of decorative paintings by *Puvis de Chavannes.*
II.—Suite of early 16th century pictures of the *Amiens School.*
III.—Collections of the City (acquired and given by the State).
IV.—Collections of the *brothers Lavalard,* given in 1890 to the City and comprising 371 pictures, including several very fine works of the French, Spanish, and Flemish schools.

1.—Paintings by Puvis de Chavannes:

These paintings decorate the walls of the grand staircase leading to the first floor, and the gallery on the first floor known as the *Puvis de Chavannes Gallery.*

1. WALLS OF THE GRAND STAIRCASE :

Work and Repose.
Ave Picardia Nutrix (1865)—*photos, p.* 41.
Pro Patria Ludus (1882), *one of the artist's masterpieces painted while he was at his very best.*

2. PUVIS DE CHAVANNES GALLERY :

The Spinner, The Reaper, The Standard-Bearer, and Desolation are four long panels between the windows. The first two relate to Peace (*Concordia*) and the other two to War (*Bellum*).

The whole of the paintings by Puvis de Chavannes, having a surface measurement of more than two hundred square yards, were removed during a violent bombardment in the spring of 1918. Sappers belonging to the "*camouflaging*" section of the army, together with firemen from Paris, carefully detached the canvases with knives and rolled them up on cylinders.

Some of them adhered so tenaciously to the walls that it was found necessary to cut away a certain thickness of stone with chisels at the same time as the canvas.

The operation was entirely successful, all the paintings being intact, with the exception of a slight tear in the "*War*" panel caused by a shell splinter, prior to removal.

It is probably in the museum of Amiens that one best realises the evolution in the decorative art of Puvis de Chavannes, as nearly a quarter of a century separates the first paintings from the last.

DETACHING THE MURAL PAINTINGS BY PUVIS DE CHAVANNES DURING THE BOMBARDMENTS IN 1918.

"PRO PATRIA LUDUS"
(FRAGMENT).
(*Cliché LL.*)

In those of the gallery, which are among the earliest of his great decorative compositions, the landscapes are a mere background of sombre hue, designed to bring out the light foreground figures. The latter are

"PRO PATRIA LUDUS"
(FRAGMENT).
(*Cliché LL.*)

individualized, the personality of each being revealed in the lines of the face and general attitude.

Conversely, in the latest works, and especially in *Pro Patria Ludus*,

"PRO PATRIA LUDUS"
(FRAGMENT).
(*Cliché LL.*)

"PRO PATRIA LUDUS"
(FRAGMENT).
(*Cliché LL.*)

the landscape is of primary importance, enveloping as it does the whole composition in a clear, pure atmosphere.

On the other hand, individuality and detail are carefully suppressed;

"AVE PICARDIA NUTRIX"
(FRAGMENT).
(*Cliché LL.*)

human beings are portrayed in their general aspect, with only the essential to characterize them.

The decorative art is here synthesized to the last degree.

"AVE PICARDIA NUTRIX"
(FRAGMENT).
(*Cliché LL.*)

PAINTING OF
OUR LADY OF
PUY (1518).
" Au juste poix
véritable
balance."

II.—Paintings of our Lady of Puy

The *Brotherhood of Our Lady of Puy* was a religious, artistic and literary society founded in the *Middle Ages* at Amiens, and which continued down to the 18th century.

The *Master*, who was elected each year, was under the obligation of having a picture painted in honour of the *Virgin*.

Several of these paintings, dating from the 16th and 17th centuries, still exist.

All are similar in composition.

In the centre, the Virgin surrounded by symbolical figures arrayed in sumptuous garments, and in the foreground, the donor with relations and friends.

Near by, a scroll inscribed with the *device* chosen by the Master for his term of office, and in the background, landscape of living waters and verdure.

The four oldest of these panels, the **wood carving** of whose *frames* is remarkable, are considered to be among the most interesting of the early 16th century French School.

The *devices* of these panels are as follows :

1. Painting (1518), No. 390 (1911 edition of catalogue) : *Au juste poix, véritable balance* ; fine Renaissance frame (*photo above*).

2. Painting (1519), No. 391 : *Pré ministrant pasture salutaire ;* Gothic-Flamboyant frame.

3. Painting (1520), No. 392 : *Palme eslute du Seigneur pour Victoire.* In the fine landscape with river, which forms the background, the city of Amiens is seen with its cathedral.

4. Painting (1521), No. 393, greatly damaged : *Le vray support de toute créature.*

The other panels are more modern and do not offer the same interest.

Several other old paintings were formerly to be found in this room, especially the central panel of a *triptych* (end 15th century), **No. 403**, representing Christ blessing, surrounded by the donor and his family, with St. John the Baptist and St. Barbara.

III.—Collections belonging to the City of Amiens

1. French School:

Boucher: Large composition; *Vénus demandant à Vulcain des armes pour Enée* (*Venus asking Vulcan for arms for Aenas*), No. 46 of 1911 catalogue.
Boucher and *Carle van Loo:* Four exquisite hunting panels, originally designed for the apartments of the King at Versailles.
Boucher: Chasse au Crocodile (*Crocodile Hunting*), dated 1739 (No. 48).
Chasse au Tigre (*Tiger Hunting*), No. 47.
Van Loo: Chasse à l'Ours (*Bear Hunting*), No. 356. *Chasse à l'Autruche* (*Ostrich Hunting*), No. 359.
Nattier: Portrait of Gresset (No. 266).
Bachelier: Two pictures forming pendants, *Un Ours de Pologne attaqué par des chiens* (*Polish bear attacked by dogs*) No. 9; *Un lion d'Afrique attaqué par des dogues* (*African lion attacked by dogs*), No. 10; and a very large composition (1761): *Les Amusements de l'enfance* (*Childhood's Amusements*), No. 8.
Quentin de la Tour: His own portrait, the finest and most carefully finished of his portraits, painted about 1760 (No. 212) (*photo below*).
David: Countess de Dillon, lady of honour to Empress Marie-Louise, full length portrait, strictly academical (No. 108).
Regnault, contemporary of David and his school: *La Mort de Priam* (*Death of Priamus*) (No. 290).
J. Lefebvre: Several paintings, especially *Portrait of Lady Godiva* (No. 223).

2. Foreign Schools:

Un buveur attablé (*Drinker at table*) (No. 427), attributed by the catalogue to the *Flemish School* of the middle of the 17th century, would seem from its powerful realism and general composition, to have come from the studio of the *Brothers Le Nain*.
Gérard de Lairesse, late 18th century, Dutch painter, now forgotten, but who enjoyed considerable notoriety in his day: *Portrait of Duchesse Marie de Clèves* (1671) (No. 206).

MAN'S PORTRAIT
BY LE GRECO.
(*Cliché LL.*)

PORTRAIT BY QUENTIN DE LA TOUR
OF HIMSELF.
(*Cliché LL.*)

IV.—Collections of the Brothers Lavalard

1. Dutch School:

Brekelenkam (1623–1688) : *Le Savetier* (*The Cobbler*) (No. 3 in 1911 catalogue).
Gerritz Cuyp (1594–1651) : *Portrait of a child*. *A Young Baron* (No. 8).
Van Goyen (1596–1696) : *Le Port de Dordrecht* (No. 12). *Le Départ pour la pêche* (*Fishing Boats setting out*) (No. 13). *Un tour au bord d'une rivière* (*River-side scene*) (No. 14, etc.).
Van Mieris (1635–1681) : *Liseuse* (*Reading*) (No. 27).
Salomon Ruysdael (1600–1670) : *Soleil couchant* (*Sunset*) (No. 38), and several other landscapes (Nos. 39 to 46).

2. Flemish School:

Franz Hals (1581–1666) : Several portraits (Nos. 94 to 96).
Brouwer (1605–1638), pupil of Franz Hals : *Un buveur* (*A Drinker*) (No. 77).
Jordaens (1593–1678) : *La Marchande de Volailles* (*Woman selling fowls*) (No. 99).
Gonzalès Coques (1614–1684) : *Exécution de Charles I. sur la place de White-Hall en 1649* (*Execution of Charles I, Whitehall*, 1649) (No. 81).

3. French School:

Louis Boily : *Un jeune Savoyard* (*Young Savoyard*) (No. 125).
Boucher : *Esquisse pour le Triomphe d'Amphitrite* (*rough sketch of Amphitrite's Triumph*) (No. 129). *Diane au bain* (*Diana taking bath*) (No. 130).
Chardin : *Lapins de garenne* (*Wild rabbits*) (No. 137), and several still-life studies (Nos. 138–140).
Fragonard : Several small paintings (Nos. 142–147), especially No. 144 : *Les Lavandières* (*Washer-Women*).
Lépicié, pupil of Carle van Loo : *Portrait de femme âgée* (*Portrait of Old Woman*) (No. 167). *Studies of children's heads* (No. 168).
Nattier : *Portrait de jeune femme* (*Portrait of a young woman*) (No. 177).
Hubert-Robert : *Colin-Maillard* (*Blindman's Buff*) (No. 188).

4. Italian School:

Luca Giordano (1632–1705) : *Musicien accordant sa guitare* (*Musician tuning his Guitar*) (No. 211).

5. Spanish School:

Le Greco (1548–1625) : Very fine *portrait of a man*, the finest of this artist's paintings in France (No. 212) (*photo p.* 43).
Ribera (1588–1656) : *La Messe du Pape Grégoire le Grand* (*Celebration of Mass by Pope Gregory the Great*) ; very finely executed ; one of this artist's greatest masterpieces ; signed : Joseph de Ribera, Naples, 1654 (No. 239).

The museum also contains *interesting drawings by Puvis de Chavannes* and a fine collection of *drawings* by the *Brothers Duthoit* of Amiens (1820–1870). In these latter drawings, more than 5,000 in number, are portrayed the *towns and villages of Picardy*, as they appeared before the disappearance of the local traditions and customs. This collection was seriously damaged by bombardment.

Several **old houses** of Amiens, saved from ruin by the Antiquarian Society of Picardy, have been rebuilt in the Museum grounds, viz. :

Late 15th century house with visible timber-work in left-hand corner.

Early 17th century (1619) façade, in right-hand corner. Note the fine decorative frieze of lions' muzzles.

Late 18th century façade, with entrance-door surmounted by a fine caryatid of bearded man supporting a graceful, wrought-iron balcony on his shoulders, against the right-hand lateral wall.

Opposite the Museum is the **Prefecture.**

The PREFECTURE consists of two contiguous buildings. One, modern, is fitted up as offices. The other, which is the Prefect's residence, was formerly the headquarters of the Intendant of Picardy.

The latter building was erected in 1773-1774 from plans prepared by the Parisian architect *Montigny*. It was considerably damaged, both outside and inside, by bombardment (*photo opposite*).

Separated from the Museum by the Rue Puvis de Chavannes is the **City Library.**

The LIBRARY is a modern building containing nearly 100,000 books and about 1,000 manuscripts, including several of great value. (*To visit apply to the curator*). The colonnaded building in the rear was partly destroyed by bombardment.

THE PREFECTURE: GREAT GALLERY.

On leaving the Rue de la République, take on the right the Rue Puvis de Chavannes (*continued by the Rue des Louvets*) as far as the Rue de Beauvais (*photo below*). Turn to the right. At the corner of the Rue de Beauvais and the Rue Frédéric-Petit is the **Lycée.**

THE LYCÉE is located in the partly rebuilt structure which was formerly the *Abbey of St. John of the Order of Premonstrants* (17th century); fine cloister.

The façade of the modern portion, looking on the Rue Frédéric-Petit, was grazed by shell splinters.

Follow the Rue de Beauvais, continued by the Rue Alphonse Leuillier, as far as the HÔTEL DE VILLE (H *on detailed plan*); 18th century façade, finished in the 19th century.

CORNER OF THE RUE DE BEAUVAIS AND RUE FRÉDÉRIC-PETIT NEAR THE LYCÉE

FAÇADE
OF THE
"BAILLIAGE."
(*Bailiwick*)

Bailliage
and
House of the
White Gable

To the left of the *Hôtel de Ville*, take the *Rue de la Malmaison*, in which is situated the **Ancien Bailliage** (Old Bailiwick — L on detailed plan). To see it, the tourist should enter the courtyard of the City Fire Station, at the bottom of which, on the right, is a narrow passage leading to a tiny court, facing which is the curious façade of the house. Gothic-Flamboyant in style, it is richly decorated with Renaissance motifs (*photos*).

A frieze of accolade-shaped arches with crockets runs along the building. Inside the arches, seven pure Renaissance medallions of men and women have been carved.

Two small Renaissance angels dated 1541 appear below, between the two rectangular windows. On the left side of the building, a pretty dormer-window with triangular pediment breaks the monotony of the large slated roof, as is customary in civil Gothic architecture. Two Renaissance medallions of a man and a woman appear on the dormer-window.

FAÇADE
OF THE
"BAILLIAGE."

Inside, interesting 16th century keel-arched timber work still exists in the audience chamber of the Bailiwick, the ceiling of which is hidden by a cloth.

Cross the Square behind the Hôtel de Ville. To the left of the Post - Office, take the Passage Gossart, at the end of which, under a vault, is the gate of a narrow alley leading to a small court.

On three sides of the latter is a curious house with wooden walls built about the year 1492 by a rich cloth merchant, Nicolas Fauvel, mayor of the city. This house, known as the **House of the White Gable**, is shown at F on the detailed plan. Abutting on the main building, which is the original structure, a kind of corbel-work gable was added over the exit from the Passage Gossart. This was probably used by the mayor as a tribune from which to harangue the people gathered together in the courtyard.

This tribune (*photo opposite*) is supported by a half-vault of wood, the arches of which abut against the stone corbels. At the outside corner, a console terminating in a flying angel forms a pendative, and is decorated with curious carving depicting a man in the dress of a 15th century burgess, having three heads.

One of his feet is bare, the other shod. On the opposite console is the figure of a man on horseback, probably Nicolas Fauvel, wearing the mayoral robes of Amiens. Part of the house with wooden walls was destroyed by a bomb, but the mayor's tribune escaped uninjured.

HOUSE OF THE WHITE GABLE.
(*Cliché L L*)

Returning to the Place de l'Hôtel de Ville, the tourist should turn to the right to see the **Ancien belfry** *of the City of Amiens (E on detailed plan).*

The lower portion only is old. Its heavy 18th century steeple contains a **bell** weighing eleven tons.

Leaving the Belfry behind, continue to follow the *Rue du Chapeau de Violettes as far as the Rue St. Germain, at the corner of which is* **St. Germain's Church** (*D on detailed plan*), historical monument. A fine building in the Flamboyant style, dating from the middle of the 15th century, it was seriously damaged by a bomb which fell in the Rue St. Germain on the night of the 13th-14th May, 1918, destroying five houses.

ST. GERMAIN CHURCH AND RUE ST.-GERMAIN.

ST.-GERMAIN
CHURCH:
DETAILS
OF PORCH.

House of the "Sagittaire"

The south façade, looking on the street, as well as that of the apse, suffered badly throughout their entire length. Although the main body of the building remained standing, most of the ornamental carving was broken and the doorway torn open, while all the stained glass was destroyed, together with the greater part of the mullions of the windows. Inside, the vaults were pierced in several places.

The doorway in the Rue Pingré is uninjured (*photo above*). Part of the ornamental carving is of great delicacy, but the statues are modern. The door is of wood with Renaissance carvings. A square tower leaning towards the North flanks the doorway.

The interior of the church is beautifully proportioned and very simple in arrangement. The choir, slightly more modern than the nave, dates from 1478. The lateral chapels contain some 16th century stained glass and a reproduction of the Burial Scene dated 1506.

Skirt the church by following the Rue St. Germain to the PLACE DU MARCHÉ DE LANSELLES (*curious old houses*).

Cross the Square diagonally on the right, then take the Rue des Vergeaux. In this street (*Nos. 57-59—K on detailed plan*) is the **Maison du Sagittaire** (*Archers' House*), so called on account of two small figures of archers carved at the top of the keystones of the arcaded vaults on the ground-floor.

HOUSE
OF THE
"SAGITTAIRE"
Rue des Vergeaux nos. 57-59.

Pure Renaissance in style and dating from 1593, it is the finest and best preserved house in the old town (*photo opposite*).

The ground-floor comprises two broken-arch arcades, each of whose tympanums is ornamented with two semi-recumbent figures of women.

A frieze ornamented with medallions of Roman warriors extends between the ground-floor and first-floor.

Five magnificent lions' muzzles appear between Renaissance motifs in this frieze.

PLACE DES HUCHERS ABOUT 1820. (*drawing by the Brothers Duthoit*).

OLD AMIENS

Return to the Place du Marché de Lanselles and take the Rue St. Martin, which is at the right-hand corner. There are two **fine façades** in this street, one Louis XV. at No. 7, and the other Louis XVI. at No. 18.

A shell caused rather serious damage to the left-hand window on the first floor of the former. *At the end of the Rue St. Martin take on the left the Rue Flatters, which continues the Rue du Bloc. Leave the latter, taking on the right the Rue des Rinchevaux which leads to the* Place des Huchers. (**Fine view** of old houses and cathedral—*photo below*).

PLACE DES HUCHERS

HOCQUET CANAL

To the right of the Square take the Rue du Pont-Piperesse visible in the photo, p. 49, then on the left, *the Rue des Gantiers and the Rue Hocquet.* At the intersection of the latter with the Rue de Metz-l'Evêque take a few steps to the right in the last-named street, to get a **view** of the picturesque Canal du Hocquet (photo above).

Continue along the Rue du Hocquet and its continuation (*Rue de la Barette*). At the end of this street, turn to the left, cross the bridge over the Somme and go up the Boulevard de Beauvillé for several hundred yards, to get a pretty **view** of the town *on the left (photo below).*

PANORAMA OF AMIENS (as seen from the Boulevard Beauvillé).

THE "HORTILLONNAGES"

THE "HORTILLON-NAGES" (KITCHEN-GARDENS).

The "Hortillonnages"

In the foreground of the above photo is a " Hortillonage." This is the local name for the tiny islets in the vicinity, whose rich black soil is generally cultivated as kitchen-gardens by men and women called " hortillons " or " hortillonnes." These gardens are intersected by innumerable small canals fed by the Rivers Somme and Avre. The most important " hortillonnages " are at the east end of the town. Visiting is only possible in the long flat-bottomed boats with turned-up ends seen in the photo above.

Each morning in summer the boats go, loaded with fruit and vegetables, to the " floating market " of Amiens (*photo below*).

The soil of these gardens is wonderfully fertile, fruit and vegetable crops succeeding one another unceasingly all the year round. The total revenue exceeds two million francs, and a " hectare "(rather less than two and a half acres) often costs twelve thousand francs.

THE "FLOATING" MARKET *Place Parmentier. In the background "Pont de la Dodane."*

THE
RUE DU DON
ON
MARKET-DAY.

The St. Leu Quarter

Return by the same way to the bridge, then turn to the right and follow the Port d'Amont as far as the first bridge (Pont du Cange). This bridge dates from the fifteenth century, and is the oldest of the many bridges which cross the canals.

Cross the bridge, then turn to the left into the Rue Belu, which runs along the river-side. From here there is a pretty **view** of the Cathedral and the old town (*photo below*). *At the end of the Rue Belu, cross the Pont de la Dodane. To the left is the Place Parmentier, where the* "Floating Market" *is held* (p. 51). *In front are the first* houses *of the* curious Rue du Don, *seen in the centre of the photo below, and on the right of the photo on p. 53.*

Take a few steps to get a good view of this street (*photo above*), *re-cross the Pont de la Dodane, then take on the left the Rue d'Engoulvent, which runs by the side of an arm of the Somme* (*photo p.* 53), *as far as the* **church of St. Leu.** *The tourist may either go round the apsis of the* church, *taking on the left the small Rue St. Leu which crosses the arm of the river, or continue straight ahead as far as the Rue St. Leu, via the Rue Graineville, which is the continuation of the Rue d'Engoulvent.*

To the right,
PONT
DE LA DODANE.
In the
background,
Place
Parmentier
entrance to the
Rue du Don.

St. Leu Church (hist. mon.) has undergone important alterations at various times. One of its façades is 15th century, and a steeple was rebuilt in the 16th century, in the Gothic style. A shell splinter broke the mullions and stained glass of one of the windows of the apse (north side). This Church is in the centre of the old quarter or lower part of the city. It is there that the commerce and industry of the town have been centralised since the Middle Ages.

A maze of narrow, winding streets crossed by innumerable canals or arms of the Somme river, connected by bridges, forms this part of the town. Numerous small water-falls supply motive power to the local factories and works. Formerly, the workshops of the fullers and dyers, which crowded the banks of the canals, and where the cloth-fulling and woad-grinding were done, were driven by water-wheels (*see p.* 2).

OLD BISHOP PALACE (*in front of Cathedral*).
To the right RUE DU DO

The houses have kept their ancient aspect, and are curious for their wooden walls, sharply pointed gables, steep roofs with tiny dormer-windows, and daring corbellings overhanging the narrow streets and canals. The only means of access to the outside which some of them possess is a foot-bridge passing over the canal.

Turn to the right into the Rue St. Leu, passing in front of the **Hôtel Dieu.** Rebuilt in the 17th and 18th centuries, except the St. John ward, which was built at the beginning of the 16th century in the Gothic-Flamboyant style, it is a spacious hall with two large roofs, the gables of which face the street. The vaulting is of wood, the ends of the beams being carved. The whole is in very bad condition.

After crossing six successive lines of canals offering picturesque perspectives (*especially the* Rue de Ville *and* Rue des Coches), *the tourist arrives at the* **Citadelle.**

The Citadelle, built in the 16th century, has since been dismantled and now serves as a barracks. The **Porte Monte-Ecu** (historical monument), built in 1531 under François I., is within its walls. It was through this Gate that the Spaniards entered Amiens in 1597. *To get a view of it, turn to the right after the Pont de la Citadelle and take the first street on the left (see detailed plan).*

Return by the same way to the Rue St. Leu. A little beyond the Church of St. Leu, take *the Rue Fernel on the right, in which several* 15th century wooden

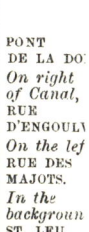

PONT DE LA DO
On right of Canal, RUE D'ENGOULV
On the left RUE DES MAJOTS.
In the background ST. LEU CHURCH.

RUE
D'ENGOULVENT
(ABOUT 1820).
(*drawing by
the Brothers
Duthoit*).

RUE DES
BOUCHERS.

houses are still to be seen. No. 33, known as the "Ramoneurs," is especially worthy of note, though greatly deteriorated.

Follow the Rue Fernel to the Place Samarobrive, to the left of which take the Rue des Bouchers (*photo below*—picturesque old houses, especially No. 33).

At the end of this street, turn to the right into the Rue Haute-des-Tanneurs, which is continued on the other side of the Place Fauvel by the Rue Basse-des-Tanneurs.

At the end of the Rue Basse-des-Tanneurs, see the ancient dilapidated façade (1493) of the **Hôtel Morgan de Belloy** (*B on detailed plan*), and the **Château d'Eau** (*A on detailed plan*), dating from the 18th century.

A natural history museum has been installed on the first floor.

From the Hôtel Morgan there is a **fine view** of the Cathedral and the lower town (*photo page 55*).

If the tourist has time he should cross the Somme by the Pont St. Michel, then follow the Boulevard du Jardin des Plantes to visit the **Jardin des Plantes**, which is on the right of the Boulevard.

Retracing his steps he should turn to the right after the Pont St. Michel, and follow the Port *d'Aval*, then turn to the left and take the Boulevard du Port.

On arriving at the **Place du Marché aux Chevaux**, turn to the right into the *Rue du Faubourg-de-la-Hotoie* as far as the **Promenade de la Hotoie** (*see coloured plan*), a magnificent *park* of about 50 acres, continued on the north by the **Jardin Anglais** of the "Petite Hotoie," ten acres in extent.

RUE BASSE DES TANNEURS seen from the Rue Condé. In the background, steeple of the Church of St. Germain and the Cathedral.

The Promenade de la Hotoie was used by the military authorities as an automobile park during the War and is now in a deplorable state.

Return via the Faubourg de la Hotoie, then take the *Rue de la Hotoie which continues it* beyond the Place du Marché aux Chevaux.

At the end of this street in the Place St. Firmin, take the *Rue St. Jacques* on the right, then immediately afterwards the *Rue Gresset* on the left (*No. 11 was formerly the* **Hôtel des Monnaies** *—18th century*).

RUE BASSE DES TANNEURS In background Hôtel Morgan and old Château d'Eau

Only the entrance door remains, the pediment of which is decorated with two fine figures of women.

Continue along the *Rue Delambre*, cross the *Place Gambetta*, and follow the *Rue des Trois Cailloux*.

After the Theatre, turn to the left into the *Rue Robert de Luzarches* which leads to the Cathedral.

HÔTEL MORGAN.

CONTENTS

	PAGES
Chief Historical Facts	2
Amiens during the War	2 to 8
Itinerary—Visit to the Town	9 to 55
The Cathedral	9 to 34
Picardy Museum	38 to 44
Old Amiens	49 to 55

OLD AMIENS

(*Drawing by the Brothers Duthoit*)

PRINTED & BOUND BY ANTONY ROWE LTD, EASTBOURNE

Printed in Great Britain
by Amazon.co.uk, Ltd.,
Marston Gate.